Cooking With Flair

by

Pietro Corsi

**Princess Cruises' cuisine
in your own kitchen**

Art Work by
Jack Manning

Published by
Princess Cruises

"Eating well depends upon two factors: the excellence of the cookery, and the competence of those who eat it."

M. Andre Maurois

Foreword

At Princess Cruises we are especially proud of our award-winning cuisine. Our Chefs prepare their dishes in the belief that cruise passengers should return home having experienced the ultimate in dining pleasure.

You will always find a variety of menu items on a Princess cruise, new dining delights and "theme" dinner nights—adventures in Italian food and mood, the ultimate in French cuisine and ambiance, choice dishes from the Caribbean and Mexico, and the splendor of Old England. We even feature a night to explore our own American heritage.

Your dining experience aboard a Princess ship can be enhanced by sharing it with your friends at home. With this booklet, you'll be able to do so—and prepare some of the elegant dishes you've enjoyed.

Moreover, our Head Waiters give cooking demonstrations on all cruises (except the shorter Party Cruises). The recipes within this booklet represent some of the dishes they demonstrate.

Buon appetito! And we look forward to seeing you again on another Princess cruise.

Pietro Corsi
Vice President,
Hotel Services

Index

Appetizers

Prosciutto and Melon 9

Ingredients:

1 ripe, medium size cantaloupe
¼ pound prosciutto, thinly sliced

PREPARATION:

Cut melon in any shape: slices, segments, cubes, or balls. Serve it with the prosciutto slices either on the melon itself, or in any other arrangement desired in the plate.

Serves 4.

Lobster Cocktail 10

Ingredients:

6 ounces boiled lobster meat, cut in small pieces
3 tablespoons diced celery hearts
3 tablespoons chopped lettuce hearts
3 tablespoons mayonnaise
2 teaspoons chili sauce
2 teaspoons Worcestershire sauce
1 tablespoon chopped chives
1 tablespoon chopped parsley
2 small tomatoes, peeled, seeded and finely chopped
1 lemon

PREPARATION:

Mix lobster with celery and lettuce. Mix together mayonnaise, chili sauce, Worcestershire sauce, chives, parsley, and tomato. Combine this dressing with the lobster mixture. Garnish each serving with a lemon wedge.

Serves 4.

Shrimp Stuffed Artichoke Hearts   *11*

Ingredients:

 2 tablespoons mayonnaise
½ pound cooked shrimp, finely diced
 2 tablespoons Triple Sec
 2 tablespoons lemon juice
½ teaspoon mustard
 1 tablespoon hot sauce
 1 scallion or shallot, finely minced
 1 can artichoke hearts
parsley, finely chopped

PREPARATION:

Combine all ingredients, except artichoke hearts. Halve the artichoke hearts. Mound with shrimp mixture. Garnish with parsley. Chill.

Serves 4/6.

Egg Canapes 12

Ingredients:

- 4 ounces mayonnaise
- 2 ounces chopped anchovies
- 1 ounce capers
- ½ teaspoon paprika
- 6 slices toasted white bread
- 2 hard boiled eggs
- 12 small artichokes in oil

PREPARATION:

Combine mayonnaise, chopped anchovies, capers and paprika in a bowl. Mix well, until creamy. Cut toast in desired shapes, and spread mixture on them. Slice hard boiled eggs and top toast with egg slice. Dot center of egg with mayonnaise mixture. Place a small opened artichoke on it. Serve (three per person) garnished with parsley.

Serves 4.

Tomatoes Stuffed with Tuna Fish　　　*13*

Ingredients:

2 large tomatoes
1 cup flaked tuna fish
3 tablespoons mayonnaise
1 teaspoon capers
spring onions
olives, salt

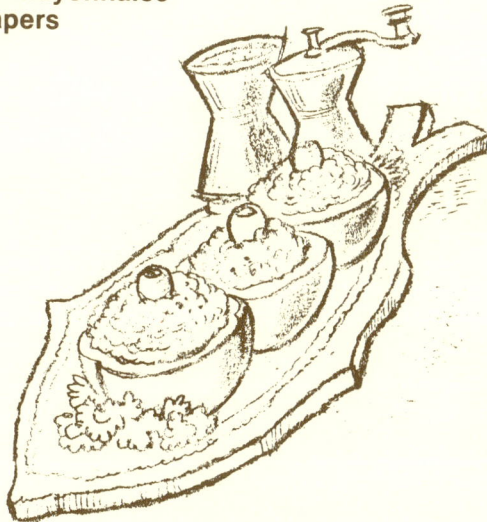

PREPARATION:

Blanch tomatoes in boiling water. Drain, sprinkle with cold water, then peel. Cut into halves and salt to taste. Place tomato halves on a sieve to drain.

Mix tuna, mayonnaise, chopped capers and spring onions in a bowl. Fill tomatoes with mixture. Top with a pitted olive. Serve tomato half per person, on a bed of lettuce. Add salt to taste.

Serves 4.

Avocado with Marinated Mushrooms   *14*

Ingredients:

2 medium avocados, ripe
12 mushrooms
2 lemons
¼ cup olive oil
2 teaspoons chili flakes
salt
pepper

PREPARATION:

Clean mushrooms, slice and place in bowl. Add salt and pepper to taste. Add olive oil, chili flakes and juice of two lemons. Marinate at least two hours. Slice avocados in half and stuff each half with mushrooms. Serve.

Serves 4.

Soups

Artichoke Cream Soup au Sherry 17

Ingredients:

4 cups chicken stock
4 onion slices
1 whole clove
1 pinch nutmeg
4 oz. canned artichoke hearts, drained
¼ teaspoon freshly ground pepper
2 tablespoons cooked rice
1 cup milk
salt
½ cup light cream
1 egg yolk
1 tablespoon sherry

PREPARATION:

In blender combine chicken stock, onion slices, clove, nutmeg, artichokes, and ground pepper. After blending, add to saucepan and
simmer for 25 minutes. Add rice and one cup scalded milk and bring
the soup to a boil. Strain the soup into another saucepan. Season it
with salt to taste, bring again to a boil, and gradually stir in the light
cream mixed with one beaten egg yolk. Before serving, stir in one
tablespoon sherry.

Serves 4.

Minestrone Genovese   18

Ingredients:

¼ lb. dried white beans
  salt
  pepper
¼ lb. potatoes
 1 stalk celery
¼ lb. zucchini
¼ lb. peas
¼ lb. green beans
¼ lb. cabbage
 2 oz. uncooked rice

PREPARATION:

Soak dried beans overnight. Cook in water, adding salt and pepper to taste. Slice all fresh vegetables and drop in boiling water. Cook over high heat one half hour. Add rice and continue cooking for another 15 to 20 minutes. Add pesto. Boil for two or three minutes and serve.

Pesto Ingredients:

6 fresh basil leaves (if dry basil is used, soak 10 min. in warm
  water)
4 oz. grated parmesan cheese
salt
2 cloves garlic
8 oz. bouillon
4 oz. olive oil

PESTO PREPARATION:

Blend basil, cheese, a pinch of salt, garlic, bouillon and olive oil. Add to minestrone, stirring well.

Serves 6 to 8.

Cream of Olive Soup   *19*

Ingredients:

½ **cup minced ripe green olives**
2 **cloves garlic**
4 **cups chicken stock**
1 **cup heavy cream**
4 **egg yolks**
salt, pepper

PREPARATION:

Simmer minced olives and garlic in chicken stock for 20 to 25 minutes. Remove garlic. Beat egg yolks and mix with heavy cream. Stir into chicken stock. Remove from heat. Season with salt and pepper to taste.

Serves 4.

Stracciatella alla Romana 20

Ingredients:

2 eggs
3 tablespoons grated Parmesan cheese
1 teaspoon minced parsley
4 cups chicken consomme
1 dash nutmeg

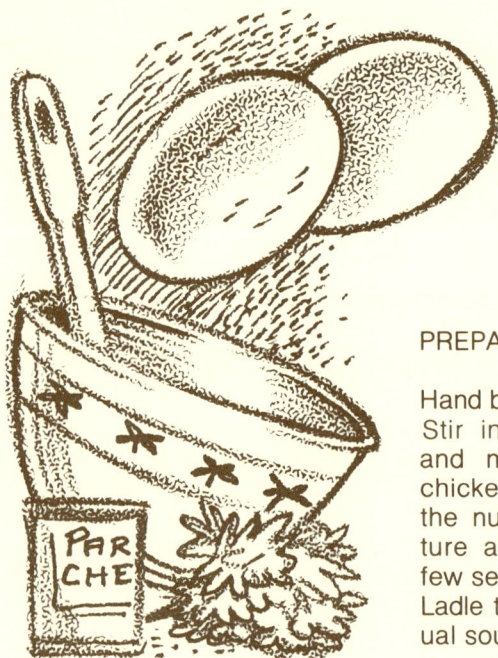

PREPARATION:

Hand beat the two eggs thoroughly. Stir in grated Parmesan cheese and minced parsley. Bring the chicken consomme to a boil. Add the nutmeg. Stir in the egg mixture and continue cooking for a few seconds, or until eggs harden. Ladle the soup at once into individual soup plates and serve.

Serves 4.

Risotto Champenois   *21*

Ingredients:

- 2 ounces butter
- ½ small onion, finely chopped
- ½ cup uncooked rice
- 1 cup Dry Champagne
- 1 cup chicken consomme
- 2 ounces heavy cream

PREPARATION:

Melt butter in a pan, add onion and let brown. Add rice, and brown. Pour champagne and let it evaporate completely on high heat while stirring constantly. Add chicken consomme at medium heat and let rice absorb it. Simmer slowly, stirring so rice doesn't stick to pan. When rice is done to taste, add the heavy cream. Mix well, letting it come to boil again. When the cream has been absorbed, the rice is ready to serve.

To be served as an entree or to accompany main dish.

Serves 4/6.

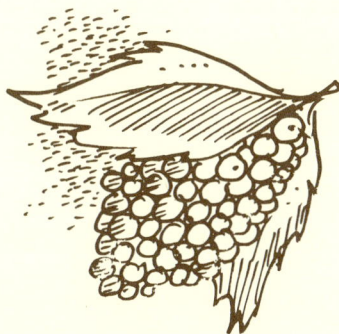

Chilled Avocado Soup 22

Ingredients:

- 1 medium onion, minced
- 1 tablespoon butter
- 1 tablespoon flour
- 2 cups chicken stock
- 1 cucumber
- 2 large avocados
- ½ cup sour cream
- salt, pepper

PREPARATION:

Using a heavy pot, saute one medium sized onion finely minced in butter until limp but not colored. Stir in the flour, pushing it around until the onion is coated. Slowly stir in 1½ cups chicken stock and slowly bring to a boil. Meantime, peel and slice cucumber, reserving a few slices for decoration, and put into blender along with the meat of avocados and ½ cup of chicken stock. Buzz until pureed. Pour into the pot with the stock and onions and heat slowly until it simmers. Chill. Season with salt and pepper to taste and serve in four individual bowls with a cucumber slice and a blob of dairy sour cream topping each.

Serves 4.

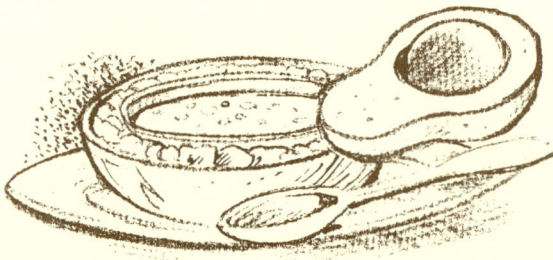

Pasta & Sauces

Pasta   25

Some say that pasta represents a typical Italian creation; others, that Marco Polo first brought it back to his native Venice from China, around 1292/96. Even the World Book Encyclopedia is not quite sure, and limits itself by saying that pasta was developed "probably" by the Chinese, with credit to the Germans and the Italians for its introduction into Europe.

Whatever its origin so many centuries ago, the fact is that pasta is now better known worldwide as a typical Italian creation, and enjoyed in its different styles, cooked in a variety of ways.

In California, we find that the best pastas are manufactured by the Costa Macaroni Mfg. Co. of Los Angeles. While it may not be available in all Supermarkets, it is freely available at Italian delicatessen stores.

Amongst the imports, we definitely find *La Molisana* to be one of the best. Produced by the Fratelli Carlone & Figli SpA in one of the smallest Regions of Italy, Molise (hence its name, Molisana), its quality is determined not only by the most modern machinery of Europe, but by the elaborate production methods which start with the most basic of ingredients: grain.

The Fratelli Carlone & Figli purchase grain at harvest time from the best producers, then pre-clean it, and store it in appropriate aging silos. After aging, the grain is cleaned and washed; then cleaned a second time, washed again and again put to rest. After a proper period of rest, the grain is ground on the premises in order to obtain, under controlled situations, the most genuine of *semolina* flour. This is subsequently stored in appropriate silos, from where, when required, it is directly drawn by the mixing machines. After mixing with the required amounts of water, so as to form a specific, pre-established degree of elasticity, the mix goes through specific machines according to the style of pasta wanted. It is worth to note that this prestigious half-century old company produces, today, well in excess of one hundred different types of pasta, from long to short, to large, to small, to smooth, to ribbed. After the pasta is thus formed, it

Pasta 26

undergoes a rapid process of drying through alternate phases of ventilation by warm air. The pasta is then ensilaged until packing time. The packing process itself is of the most automated, and consists of the weighing, the automatic forming of the packaging wrapper according to the desired weight, the filling and sealing of the individual packs, which are then transferred, always automatically, to a bulk machine which places the packs in cartons, while at the same time sealing them. And the cartons are ready for shipment throughout Europe and worldwide.

Now that you know how pasta is manufactured, we will tell you how to cook it and then, how to prepare the different varieties of sauces—some of which you will have tasted during your Princess cruise.

Ingredients:

½ lb. pasta
4/6 quarts water
1 tbsp. salt

PREPARATION:

Bring salted water to a boil. Cook pasta of your choice for 6/10 minutes, or until "al dente" (slightly under-cooked.) Cooking time will vary depending on the type of pasta used, and the brand. We suggest that you start tasting your pasta after the first six minutes, and every minute after until cooked to taste. Remove the pasta from water and drain well. You should avoid pre-cooking the pasta, and setting it aside for too long before adding to the sauce. Half a pound of pasta is sufficient for 4.

Sauces for Pasta

There are a number of sauces that can be used to complement pasta, and we will indicate which goes better with what type of pasta.

Every Chef or Maitre d'Hotel the world over will have his own "very special" sauce. However, the basic ingredients are practically universal. In addition to the ingredients given by whatever recipe, you can add your own imagination and rest assured of the good results.

Nobody would have tried, for instance, Pasta with Curry Sauce until our own Chefs dared . . . and they are now sharing their recipe with you.

Each of the following recipes is sufficient for 4.

Scarpara Sauce

Ingredients:

¼ cup olive oil
3 cloves garlic, chopped
1 teaspoon chopped capers
oregano
1 pound peeled tomatoes
1 teaspoon crushed pepper
minced parsley
grated Parmesan cheese
salt
3 black olives chopped
3 green olives chopped

PREPARATION:

In a skillet, heat oil. Add garlic and let it fry until light-golden. Add all other ingredients and salt to taste. Cook for 15 to 20 minutes. Add the pasta and blend well with grated Parmesan cheese. Serve.

Type of pasta suggested: Spaghetti.

Clam Sauce

Ingredients:

2 ounces butter
1 small chopped onion
2 cloves of garlic, chopped
1 cup clam broth
10 ounces fresh clams, diced. If using canned clams,
   drain well
1 cup flour
1 teaspoon oregano
4 ounces canned red peppers, diced
1 tablespoon chopped parsley
½ cup heavy cream
salt
pepper

PREPARATION:

In a skillet, melt butter at low heat. Add the chopped onion. When golden, add the chopped garlic and cook for a minute. Add the clam broth, and bring to boil. Dip the diced clams in the flour, then add them to the skillet. Mix well, and let cook for 5 minutes at low heat. Add oregano, diced pepper, parsley, and mix well. Add cream, salt and pepper to taste. After blending well, mix in the pasta and you are ready to serve. Preferably, no Parmesan cheese is added to this sauce.

Type of pasta suggested: Spaghetti.

Crabmeat Sauce 30

Ingredients:

1 ounce olive oil
1 medium onion diced
2 cloves garlic diced
1 tablespoon parsley finely chopped
½ pound flaked crabmeat
3 ounces white wine
2 cups peeled tomatoes
salt, pepper

PREPARATION:

Heat oil in a skillet. Add onion and cook until golden. Add garlic, parsley and crabmeat. Cook for 10 minutes at medium heat. Stir in white wine and let it evaporate. Add the peeled tomatoes and cook at low heat for 30 minutes. Add salt and pepper to taste. Mix in the pasta, and serve. No Parmesan cheese is required for this sauce.

Type of pasta suggested: Spaghetti or Linguine.

Bolognese Sauce 31

Ingredients:

1 ounce butter
2 tablespoons olive oil
1 clove garlic
1 medium onion, diced
1 stalk celery, diced
1 small carrot, diced
1 teaspoon chopped parsley
½ ounce dried, diced mushrooms pre-soaked in hot water
½ pound ground beef
¼ pound ground pork
2 ounces ham, finely diced
2 ounces mortadella, finely diced
4 ounces red wine
½ pound peeled, chopped tomatoes
1 laurel leaf
1 tablespoon flour
2 cups beef stock or gravy
1 tablespoon tomato paste
salt, pepper
grated Parmesan cheese

PREPARATION:

Over low heat, place the butter and the olive oil in a skillet. Add garlic, onion, celery and carrot. Increase heat to medium high. Add parsley and mushrooms. Cook for 2 minutes. Add beef, pork, ham and mortadella, and raise heat. Mix well until cooked. Stir in red wine and let it evaporate. Add the peeled tomatoes, laurel leaf, flour, and stir well while adding the beef gravy or stock. Reduce heat to low, add tomato paste and cook for approximately one hour. Add salt and pepper (and a dash of nutmeg, if desired). Place the pasta in the skillet, and blend well with Parmesan cheese. You are ready to serve. It is desirable to have butter on the table for your Guests to add some to their individual serving of pasta for a better blend.

Type of pasta suggested: Practically any type, but particularly good for spaghetti, rigatoni, mostaccioli.

Puttanesca (or Southern) Sauce 32

Ingredients:

2 ounces olive oil
1 small onion, diced
2 cloves garlic, diced
1 tablespoon parsley, finely chopped
1 tablespoon capers
1 dozen mixed green and black olives, halved
1 teaspoon oregano
4 each diced anchovies
3 ounces white wine
1 cup tomato sauce
salt, pepper

PREPARATION:

Place oil and onion in a skillet, at medium heat. When the onion is lightly browned, add garlic, parsley, capers, olives, oregano and anchovies. Cook slowly for about three minutes. Stir in white wine. Let evaporate. Add the tomato sauce, and cook for 10 minutes. Add pasta to the skillet, and mix well with or without grated Parmesan cheese at your pleasure.

Type of pasta suggested: Spaghetti.

Curry Sauce 33

Ingredients:

2 ounces butter
1 small onion, diced
3 ounces julienne of ham
2 ounces cream cheese
4 ounces heavy cream
2 peeled tomatoes, diced
1 tablespoon curry powder
salt
pepper
grated Parmesan cheese

PREPARATION:

Place butter and onion in a skillet at medium heat. Lightly brown onion. Add ham, cream cheese, heavy cream and tomato paste. Mix well. Add the curry powder, salt and pepper to taste. Cook until the cream cheese is melted. Add the pasta to the skillet, and blend well with sufficient grated Parmesan cheese.

Type of pasta suggested: Spaghetti, or short maccaroni.

Carbonara Sauce 34

Ingredients:

5 strips of bacon, chopped
4 egg yolks
1 cup cream
grated Parmesan cheese
3 ounces butter
Salt
Pepper

PREPARATION:

Fry the chopped bacon, and set aside. Place the egg yolks, cream and grated Parmesan cheese in bowl stirring well. Set aside. Melt the butter in pan at medium heat. Add the chopped bacon, and re-heat until bacon and butter become frothy. Add the pasta to the pan, stirring constantly. Pour the egg mixture over pasta, stirring well. Add salt and pepper to taste, if desired. Serve.

Type of pasta suggested: Spaghetti.

Caruso Sauce   35

Ingredients:

6 oz. chicken livers
1 lemon
2 oz. butter or olive oil
2 cloves garlic
6 oz. tomato puree
2 fresh basil leaves (or one teaspoon dry basil)
salt
pepper

PREPARATION:

Cut chicken livers in small pieces. Clean them well and wash in bowl of cold water containing juice of lemon. Drain and pat dry with paper towel.

Heat shortening in pan and add garlic, finely minced. Allow it to brown, then add chicken livers. Cook over high heat for 4 minutes. Stir in tomato puree and basil. Simmer a couple of minutes. Add salt and pepper to taste. Mix well into pasta.

Type of pasta suggested: Noodles (or rice).

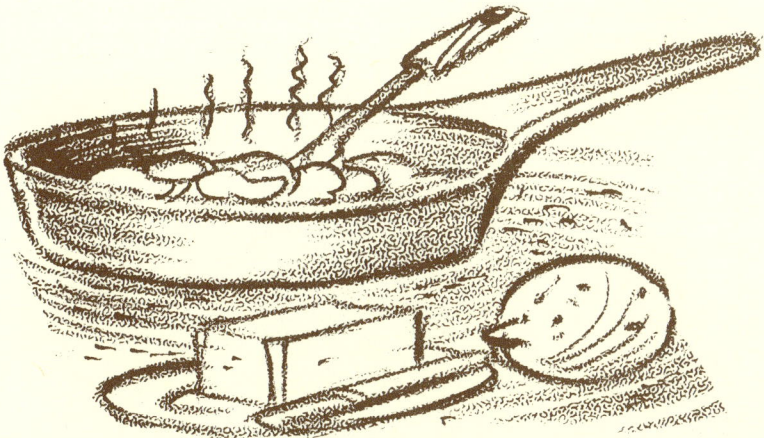

Fish

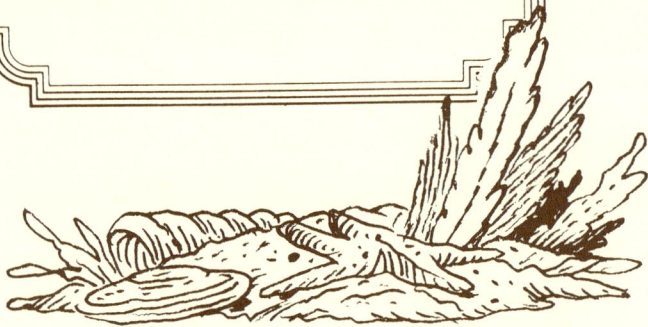

Shrimp Flambe', Newburg   **39**

Ingredients:

2 tablespoons butter
1 Spanish onion, chopped
12 each raw jumbo shrimps deveined
2 jiggers brandy
1 cup heavy cream
1 egg yolk
1 teaspoon chopped parsley
a dash of Cayenne pepper
salt

PREPARATION:

In skillet melt butter and saute onions until brown. Add shrimp and cook for ten minutes over medium heat. Add brandy, and flame. Cook until flame goes out. Blend together cream, egg yolk, parsley and Cayenne pepper. Add to shrimps. Stir well without letting sauce thicken. Add salt to taste. Serve hot with rice pilaff.

Serves 4.

Rice Pilaff

Ingredients:

½ cup long-grained rice, uncooked
2 ounces butter
1 medium onion
2 cloves
1 clove garlic
½ teaspoon saffron
2 cups bouillon
salt

PREPARATION:

Wash one cup long-grained rice several times. Soak it for 2 hours, and drain. Melt butter in a deep, heavy pan. Add onion pierced with cloves. Add garlic clove and saute until onion and garlic are soft and translucent. Add rice, stirring occasionally for 5 to 6 minutes. Add salt to taste. Add half a teaspoon of saffron to the bouillon and simmer 10 minutes. Bring bouillon to a boil. Add it to the rice, covering it approximately one inch. Cover the pan tightly and cook rice over low heat for 20 minutes, or until bouillon is absorbed, and rice is tender.

Trout Flambe' au Chablis   *40*

Ingredients:

**4 trout, 8 to 10 ounces each
4 ounces butter
1 tablespoon French Mustard (Dijon)
Perrin's sauce
Tabasco sauce
2 ounces Chablis wine
1 tablespoon heavy cream
3 ounces tomato puree
salt, pepper
2 ounces Cognac**

PREPARATION:

Clean, wash and dry trout. Fillet them. Place butter in a heated pan and melt. Add French mustard and blend well. Add a few drops of Perrin's sauce and Tabasco sauce to taste, and blend well. Pour in the Chablis and let evaporate. Add heavy cream pre-mixed with tomato puree. When this is blended with sauce, add the fillets of trout. Add salt and pepper to taste. Cook for about 10 minutes. Pour in the Cognac, and flame. When the flame is out, place the fillets of trout in a serving dish. Pour remaining sauce on them and serve.

Serves 4.

Trout Champenoise   *41*

Ingredients:

    4 trout, 8 to 10 ounces each
    3 ounces butter
    2 cloves garlic
    salt, pepper
    1 split Dry Champagne
    1 teaspoon flour
2½ ounces heavy cream
    3 egg yolks

PREPARATION:

Clean, wash and dry trout. Place 2 ounces butter in pan. Add garlic cloves, brown, and remove. Dip in trout and fry for a few minutes while adding the salt and pepper to taste. Add Champagne. Let cook for about 10 minutes. Remove trout and place in serving dish. When the juice in the pan is reduced, add the remaining butter previously mixed with flour. Cook for a minute or two. Pour in the heavy cream. When the sauce is hot blend it with the egg yolks. Pour on the trout and serve.

Serves 4.

Scampi Fra' Diavolo Flambe'

Ingredients:

4 ounces butter
1 clove garlic
2 pounds Scampi (or Gulf Prawns)
1 tablespoon French Mustard (Dijon)
Perrin's sauce
Tabasco sauce
2 ounces Sherry
1 large tomato, peeled, chopped
salt, pepper
2 ounces Cognac
2 tablespoons chopped parsley

PREPARATION:

In pan, melt butter with garlic. When the garlic is brown, remove and add scampi. Cook at medium heat for about five minutes. Remove from pan. Add mustard to pan and blend well with butter. Add a few drops of Perrin's sauce and Tabasco sauce. Pour in Sherry, and blend for a minute or two. Add chopped tomato and blend. Replace the scampi in pan, and cook for another five minutes. Add salt and pepper to taste. Pour Cognac over scampi, and flame. Serve, preferably on a bed of rice and pour remaining sauce on scampi. Sprinkle with minced parsley.

Serves 4.

Golden Fillet of Sole, Pecan   *43*

Ingredients:

**1 pound fillet of sole
juice of one lemon
1 cup flour
2 egg yolks
2 cups breadcrumbs
1 cup pecans, chopped
4 ounces butter
salt, pepper**

PREPARATION:

Marinate fillet of sole for 15 minutes in lemon juice, salt and pepper. Place the flour in a dish, the beaten egg yolks in a bowl, and the breadcrumbs and pecans mixed in another dish. Dip the fillet in flour, in egg yolk, and in the breadcrumbs mixture. Melt butter in a pan. Saute the fillet for about 10 minutes. Add salt and pepper to taste. Serve.

Serves 4.

Meat

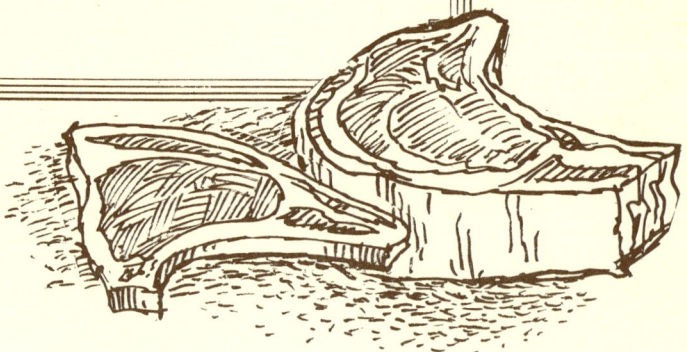

Steak Diane

Ingredients:

    2 ounces butter
    4 tenderloins of beef (6 to 8 ounces each), thinly flattened
    2 ounces shallots
    4 ounces sliced champignons
    2 ounces Cognac
 ½ cup beef stock
    2 tablespoons heavy cream
    Salt, pepper

PREPARATION:

Melt butter in one skillet. Brown steaks on both sides and set aside. In second skillet, gently brown shallots and champignons in butter. Add steaks, heat well and flambe' with Cognac. When flame is out, add beef stock, cream, salt and pepper. Turn steaks a couple of times for 3 or 4 minutes each side at high heat. When sauce thickens, serve.

Serves 4.

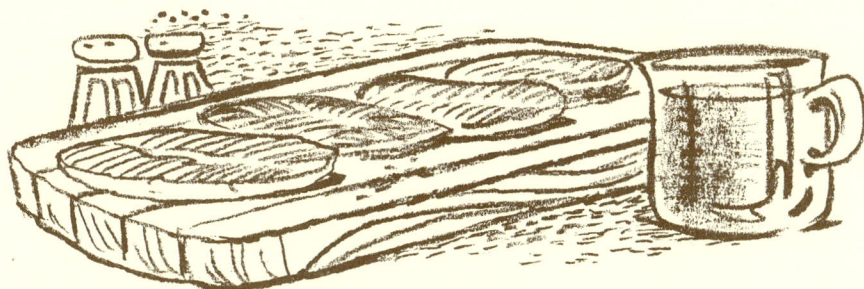

Veal Scaloppine, Marsala   *48*

and Mushroom Sauce

Ingredients:

1 pound veal, in small flattened pieces
1 cup flour
Salt, pepper
2 ounces butter
4 ounces Marsala wine
2 ounces meat gravy
8 ounces sliced mushrooms
chopped parsley

PREPARATION:

Place veal in flour and sprinkle with salt and pepper to taste. In pan, melt butter and brown veal on both sides. As veal is turned, sprinkle with Marsala wine and let evaporate. Remove veal from pan. Add a little Marsala, butter, meat gravy, salt and pepper to pan. Cook for a few minutes. Add mushrooms and cook until tender. Pour sauce on the scaloppine, sprinkle with parsley and serve.

Serves 4.

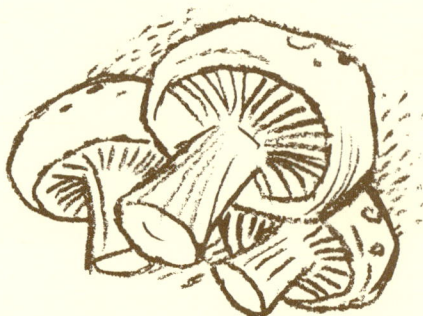

Veal Piccata Lombarda   *49*

Ingredients:

1 pound veal in small, flattened pieces
½ cup flour
salt, pepper
3 ounces butter
 juice of 2 lemons
chopped parsley

PREPARATION:

Place veal in flour, and sprinkle with salt and pepper to taste. Melt 1½ ounces butter in pan. Add veal, browning on both sides. Add lemon juice and balance of butter while stirring. Sprinkle with parsley. Serve (with mashed potatoes) and pour remaining sauce over the veal.

Serves 4.

Karib-Kebab Flambe' 50

Ingredients:

- ½ cup pineapple juice
- 2 tablespoons dark molasses
- ¼ cup vinegar
- 2 tablespoons olive oil
- 1 tablespoon salt
- 1 teaspoon black, freshly ground pepper
- 2 pounds beef sirloin, in 1½" cubes
- 12 spring onions
- 2 green bell peppers, in 1½" cubes
- 12 cherry tomatoes
- ½ pineapple, in 1½" cubes
- 2 ounces Jamaican rum

PREPARATION:

In glass bowl, mix pineapple juice, molasses, vinegar, olive oil, salt, pepper and cubes of beef. Marinate one hour. Clean and peel onions, and place in boiling water for 10 to 12 minutes. Pierce on four skewers, alternating bell pepper cubes with tomatoes, beef cubes, pineapple cubes and so on. Place skewers on a grill at medium heat. Cook slowly, rotating skewers often while basting with remaining marinade. When meat is ready to taste, flame in Jamaican Rum (or Cognac, if desired) and serve, preferably on a bed of rice.

Serves 4.

Fillet of Beef New Orleans, Flambe'

Ingredients:

2 ounces butter
2 laurel leaves
1 tablespoon French mustard (Dijon)
2 tablespoons chopped parsley
3 ounces tomato sauce
½ cup diced green bell pepper
½ cup chopped mushrooms
Perrin's sauce
Tabasco sauce
2 ounces Sherry
salt, pepper
4 tenderloins of beef, 6/8 ounces, 1" thick
2 ounces Cognac

PREPARATION:

Melt butter in pan. Add laurel leaves, French mustard, chopped parsley, tomato sauce, diced bell pepper, chopped mushrooms, and blend.
Add a few drops of Perrin's sauce and Tabasco sauce. Sprinkle in
sherry and let evaporate. Add salt and pepper to the fillets, and place
in pan. Cook for three to four minutes or to taste. Pour in Cognac
and flame. Cook a few more minutes. Place the fillets on a serving
plate and pour remaining sauce on them. Serve.

Serves 4.

Lamb Cutlets, Brandy Sauce 52

Ingredients:

   12 lamb cutlets
   1 cup flour
   2 ounces margarine
1½ ounces brandy
   2 ounces cream cheese
2½ ounces milk
   1 cup beef stock

PREPARATION:

Flatten cutlets then dip in flour.
Melt margarine in large pan and
brown cutlets. Sprinkle with brandy
and let evaporate. In a separate
bowl, dilute cream cheese with
milk and the beef stock. Pour this
mixture on cutlets, and cover pan.
Cook cutlets for 10 to 15 minutes
at low heat, turning occasionally.
When cutlets are cooked, place
in serving dish and pour remaining
sauce over them. Serve.

Serves 4.

Desserts

Bananas Flambe'   *55*

Ingredients:

  4 medium size firm bananas
  4 tablespoons granulated sugar
  1 cup flour
  2 eggs
  2 tablespoons butter
  2 ounces Kirsh

PREPARATION:

Peel bananas, cut them in half lengthwise and sprinkle with sugar. Dip in flour, then in beaten eggs and again in flour. Saute in butter until lightly brown on both sides. Bananas should be soft, not mushy. Arrange on warm serving platter and sprinkle with sugar. Pour Kirsh over, ignite and serve flaming.

Serves 4.

Zabaglione

Ingredients:

6 egg yolks
1 egg white
6 tablespoons sugar
3 ounces Marsala wine
½ cup whipped cream
½ cup shaved chocolate
4 ladyfingers

PREPARATION:

In the top of a double boiler, beat egg yolks, egg white and sugar. When the mixture is very thick and creamy add Marsala wine. Place the pan over simmering water, heating the mixture gradually while constantly beating. When the Zabaglione is very thick and hot, spoon into four stemmed glasses. Top with whipped cream. Garnish with shaved chocolate. Serve with one ladyfinger.

Serves 4.

Cherries Jubilee   *57*

Ingredients:

4 tablespoons granulated sugar
Juice of one orange
Juice of one lemon
1 can dark pitted cherries
1 ounce Maraschino
2 ounces Cherry Herring, or Kirsh
4 scoops vanilla ice cream
whipped cream
4 tablespoons chopped almonds

PREPARATION:

Melt sugar in pan at medium high heat. Add orange and lemon juices, stirring well, until sauce thickens. Add drained cherries and Maraschino. Cook for ten minutes at high heat. Pour Cherry Herring or Kirsh over the cherries and ignite. Serve in four dishes over scoop of vanilla ice cream. Top with whipped cream. Sprinkle with chopped almonds.

Serves 4.

Crepes Suzette   58

(a) Preparing Batter
Ingredients:
- 2 eggs
- 6 tablespoons milk
- ¼ teaspoon vanilla
- ½ teaspoon sugar
- 2 tablespoons all-purpose flour
- 1 pinch salt
- 1 teaspoon butter

Beat the eggs thoroughly. Add milk, vanilla and sugar. Sift flour with salt. Add to egg mixture. Beat until smooth. In a very small chafing dish, heat butter. Drop one tablespoon of batter into chafing dish. Brown both sides lightly, remove from pan and set aside. Prepare remaining batter accordingly.

(b) Preparing Crepes Suzette
Ingredients:
- 6 cubes sugar
- 2 orange peels
- 2 lemon peels
- 4 tablespoons granulated sugar
- 1 ounce sweet butter, softened
- juice of 2 medium oranges, freshly squeezed, strained
- 2 ounces Grand Marnier
- 8-12 crepes, prepared as above
- ½ lemon
- 2 ounces Cognac

Rub sugar cubes into one orange peel and one lemon peel so that oil of fruit penetrates the cubes (white inner rind should be removed first).

Place granulated sugar in chafing dish and melt until lightly brown. Add sugar cubes and butter. Stir until cubes are melted and well blended. Add orange juice, remaining orange and lemon peels, Grand Marnier, and stir until thickened. Place crepes in chafing dish, warming on each side. Fold in half twice, and cook until warmed through. Squeeze the lemon on crepes. Raise heat and when chafing dish is very hot, pour Cognac over crepes and ignite. When the flame dies, serve crepes in a hot dish. Pour remaining juice over crepes. Serve.

Serves 4.

Italian Tipsy Cake   *59*

Ingredients:

3 layers spongecake, approximately ¾" thick and 9" diameter
1 cup rum
2 cups fruit preserves
4 cups vanilla or chocolate custard
2 cups whipped cream
½ cup assorted candied fruits

PREPARATION:

Place one layer of spongecake on large serving plate and sprinkle with ½ cup rum. Spread it with one cup of your favorite fruit preserves. Pour two cups of the custard over the preserves. On this, place the second layer of spongecake and spread with same amounts of preserves and custard (no rum). Add the third layer of cake and impregnate with remaining rum. Top with whipped cream, candied fruits and serve.

Serves 12.

Amaretti

Ingredients:

½ pound almond paste (may be purchased in cans)
1 cup plus 2 tablespoons very fine granulated sugar
2 egg whites

PREPARATION:

Cut almond paste into small pieces. Combine with sugar and egg whites. Work the mixture well until free of any lumps. With a spoon, shape mixture into rounds about one inch wide. Drop onto greased baking sheet, leaving spaces between rounds for paste to spread. Bake at 325°F for about 15 to 20 minutes. Remove from baking sheet before they are completely cooled.

Acknowledgements

This collection of recipes was made possible by the cooperation and contribution of our Chefs Pino Traverso, Derek Ellison, Paolo Bonanno, Giovanni Verda, Malcolm Pearce and Mario Rotti. My thanks to each of them.

Considerable time in the experimentation of most recipes was also contributed by Head Waiter Giuseppe Barbini and his team of Head Waiters of Sun, Island and Pacific Princess.

Finally, the publication would not have been possible without the patience of my assistant Carole Hartel, whose task it was to put the puzzle together.

Pietro Corsi

Notes